MY DAD WAS SO MEAN

by

ELIZABETH STREB PARKS

Illustrated by

David Phillip Parks

Copyright © 2017 Elizabeth Streb Parks and David Phillip Parks.

All rights reserved, including the right to reproduce this book, or portions thereof, in any form. No part of this text may be reproduced, transmitted, downloaded, decompiled, reverse engineered, or stored in or introduced into any information storage and retrieval system, in any form or by any means, whether electronic or mechanical without the express written permission of the author. The scanning, uploading, and distribution of this book via the Internet or via any other means without the permission of the publisher is illegal and punishable by law. Please purchase only authorized electronic editions and do not participate in or encourage electronic piracy of copyrighted materials.

Cover and Interior Illustrations: Copyright © David Phillip Parks

Published by: Telemachus Press, LLC
http:// www.telemachuspress.com

ISBNs
978-1-945330-18-6 (eBook)
978-1-945330-76-6 (hard cover)

10 9 8 7 6 5 4 3 2 1

20220610

In Loving Memory of
my mom and dad, Ann and Verne Streb

CHAPTER ONE

It should be against the law. In fact, it probably was. But my dad did it anyway: he picked me up and hung me over the rail at Niagara Falls. And everybody laughed, except me and my mom, Ann. She said, "Verne, stop that! You're scaring her!"

Since it was a hot day, I didn't mind the cooling mist gently caressing my body, as I glanced over my shoulder and looked down upon the massive, roaring waterfalls. All five of my brothers laughed and said, "Drop her, Dad!" or "Give her a shower!"

In the meantime, I just sort of swung in the wind, hanging on and looking up into my dad's laughing brown eyes. Then he pulled me up and over, and I never cried, but just ran to my mom for a comforting hug and a shared knowledge: males bond by scaring females.

When we first arrived in Buffalo, New York, it was December. As our train pulled into the station, I was anxious to get off and go play in the snow that I had been watching from the fast moving train windows for at least an hour. It was a heavy blizzard, and normal for Buffalo, but not for our family.

After the train came to a complete stop, my father took me by the hand and led me to the door of the passenger compartment. Then he picked me up and stepped down to the swept pavement below. He walked over to where all the snow had fallen and placed me into the midst of it. The snow was up to my chest!

As my five brothers all piled off the train and saw my dad using me to measure how deep the snow was, they all started laughing hysterically. It must have looked pretty funny, seeing the shoulders and head of this little red-haired, blue-eyed girl sticking out of the snow. But when my mom came down the steps and saw me, she said, "Now Verne! Get her out of that snow! She's going to get pneumonia!"

Since the snow was so deep and still falling, there was no way we could drive out to our new home, so we were stuck spending the night at a hotel near the railroad station, a great adventure to six kids traveling for the first time. There was only one problem: the whole family had to stay in one room, with one double bed and two chairs! Talk about a close family!

Not only was the room sparingly furnished, but the decor could be described as boring basic beige. The heavy drapes were beige, the ceiling was beige, and the wallpaper was a beige pattern, with tiny pink roses climbing the wall. However, we were not there for decorating tips, but for sleep.

My mom always remembered it as the worst night of her life. After several hours of trying to corral all my brothers on the train, she then had to spend her first night in New York sitting upright in an uncomfortable chair. My dad had no trouble sleeping in the other matching chair, and his loud snores soon reverberated throughout the strange room. All six of us kids were lined up like sardines in the bed, lying parallel to the headboard and footboard, tightly packed and ready for sleep. I take that back … five kids were ready for sleep, since the excitement of the big trip had exhausted them, and they sensed the urgent need to recharge their batteries for the coming day. But one kid had already recharged his batteries on the train with a long nap, and he was rarin' to go.

So as Ralph, Billy, David, Bobby and I, Betty Jean, tried to rest our weary bones, brother Donny had other ideas. He climbed on top of the footboard and posed like a world-class diver. Then he leaped into the air and landed on top of a bunch of flailing bodies, as hollers and yelps filled the air. Donny laughed with pure joy at his newly discovered activity, until my mom sternly said, "Donny! Stop that immediately and go to sleep!"

So Donny crept over our bodies back to his place at the foot of the bed and quietly rested for a few minutes. Then, just as we were all settling into the snooze state … KABOOM! He did it again! And this time our cries woke the sleeping giant: Dad.

"What's going on?!" he bellowed.

All six of us were explaining and complaining at the same time, so that a clear response turned into mass confusion. Finally, Dad yelled, "Enough! Now everybody get to sleep! And I mean NOW!"

Immediately, the tense atmosphere went silent, for a few moments, at least. To this day, I don't know who started it, who broke the silence. But one of us started to giggle, and giggling being contagious, within a few minutes, we were out of control with laughter.

Again, Dad yelled, "Quiet!"

An attempt was made to be quiet and serious, but it was too late. We tried not to make a sound. Honest, we did! But there's one thing worse than giggling and that's trying not to giggle. So there we were, six bodies lined up like slats on a picket fence, trying to control something uncontrollable: contagious laughter. Our bodies shook silently, our eyes teared, and snorts escaped our noses. When we could stand it no longer, we burst into laughter and Donny took one more leap. This time we all grabbed him and had an impromptu wrestling session, peals of laughter rising from the bed. Even Mom and Dad were laughing heartily. And that's how we spent our first night in New York.

CHAPTER TWO

As we settled into normal life in Buffalo, or rather a rural area about ten miles to the southwest, my brothers were in boy heaven. After being raised their entire lives in an apartment in a city in Ohio, they now had a big, old farmhouse and hundreds of acres to roam. There were two large barns, an orchard, a pond and a beautiful woods to explore, and one mile away was their favorite thing: Lake Erie. Being the only girl with five brothers offered me two options: I could stay home with the only feminine influence in my young life, my mom, and learn to cook the food, clean the house, wash, dry, iron and sew the clothes … and shop. Or I could hang out with the feisty five who intended to explore our new world with the curiosity of Christopher Columbus. Of course, I joined the search and discover crew.

So as my mom kept busy in her job of taking care of a home and the daily needs of a family of eight, and my dad kept busy in his job at a steel mill, financially supporting the home and the family of eight, we six adventurers also had a job to do, and that was to have as much fun as we could every day.

A lot of that fun involved snow, which we prayed for nightly from October on, so that the schools would be closed. Those years our prayers were answered often, and we would become Admiral Byrd and his team of Antarctic explorers. My brothers built a wonderful igloo, quite large by igloo standards. After crawling through the opening, we could stand up inside our own private, cool, white round room. Then they built a second one and called them forts. The rest of the day, supplies of snowballs were made and stored for future use. One never knew when the enemy would walk in the vicinity and need to be taught a lesson: don't mess with Antarctic explorers. After throwing a few snowballs

the enemy's way and getting a great response, whether screams by passing girls, or yells by passing boys, they'd start pelting each other with the snowy missiles, and I would make a quick getaway into an igloo.

The next day, my brothers gave me a special assignment: build a snowman to guard the igloo, while they built a snowman to guard the other igloo. Rolling the ball which was to be the foundation for my snowman was a strategic endeavor, and I wanted it to be just the right size. But when I felt sure it was the perfect size and shape, I realized I was far away from the igloos, and I decided to move the huge ball by putting it on my sled and giving the snowman's bottom a ride to the igloo area. Knowing nothing yet about physics and the concept of weight and power and distance, I wrapped my arms and mittened hands around the gigantic snow mass, and I lifted with all my heart and strength. Then I felt my insides actually break or tear, and the pain was excruciating as I let out a scream and fell to the ground, holding my stomach so it wouldn't come out of me!

My screams continued and my brothers came running to see what had happened, what or who had hurt me. Then my mother came running out of the house, without a coat or boots, followed by my dad, in his grey long underwear and brown leather slippers.

"Who hurt her?!" my dad bellowed, as my mom gently took me into her arms and said, "What happened, Honey?"

All five brothers declared their innocence and also their ignorance; they didn't have a clue as to why I was crying out in such obvious pain. Their faces looked so concerned and confused, and my dad just got angrier, demanding answers. My oldest brother, Ralph, defended them by declaring, "We don't know anything! We told her to make a snowman to guard the igloo, and she was making it just fine. Then she started screaming!"

Gently transferring my sobbing body to my dad, my parents made their way through the deep snow and made their way into the house, followed by the confused cluster of baffled boys. When my agony didn't subside, and my dad had dressed, they rushed me to the hospital.

At the hospital in downtown Buffalo, the doctor questioned my parents as to the cause of my agony and, of course, they responded that it was a mystery to them. Upon further examination, the doctor asked if I had picked up anything heavy.

"No, not really," I answered sobbingly. "I tried to pick up my snowman's bottom to put it on my sled so I could move it nearer to the igloos. But then I felt my tummy break!"

The doctor admitted me to the hospital, and that's where I spent Christmas vacation that year … Our Lady of Victory Hospital, having a hernia operation. My mom and dad visited daily, but my brothers had to stay at home. This was one adventure I had to experience on my own, and I didn't like it one bit!

My homecoming was a celebration worthy of a returning hero, for none of my brothers had been to a hospital since birth, and I had gone into an uncharted territory alone and endured a procedure involving cutting me open and sewing me back up again. They were in awe and nicer than usual. But my dad seemed a little bit crankier.

CHAPTER THREE

In the spring, after a full recuperation, I again joined the fearless five. Walking in the neighboring orchard under the blossom-filled trees, we felt like we had entered an enchanted land, with a magical roof of pink and white fragrant flowers extending forever, bordered by forsythia, lilac and snowball bushes. The natural beauty was intoxicating and we all drank it into our souls, like desert wanderers at an oasis. That first spring we had no idea which trees would bear apples, or cherries, peaches, plums or pears. We were just satisfied with drinking in the beauty of the blossoms.

No longer hampered by the slippery snow, we could hardly wait to climb the trees. To sit in a blossoming cherry tree, or peach tree, or apple tree was to preview a seat in heaven. After climbing the various trees for a few days, my brother Bobby decided to take his quest for heights to a new level. With the five of us as an engrossed audience, he proceeded to put on a show.

Using the back-porch rail, he climbed to the porch roof, where he put on a little act with a promised surprise ending. All my brothers were thin and tall for their ages, especially Ralph and Bobby, who both wore glasses, since they were extremely nearsighted. Straight light-brown hair topped Bobby's head, and a cowlick crowned the back center. Being the fourth boy born, he rarely wore new clothes … only hand-me-downs. This day he wore a blue and red striped short sleeve polo shirt and blue jeans, still a little too large and held up by red suspenders.

After telling a few silly jokes, he said he was not going to climb back down; he was going to parachute to the ground! Wow! That sounded exciting and we all cheered Bobby on to do it. I don't know how it got up there on the top of a roof, but there it was … an umbrella. To Bobby, that was the same as a parachute, if not better. With great style and showmanship, he opened the umbrella, took a few steps nearer to the edge of the roof, and then he jumped!

Oh, what a beautiful sight it was, at least at the beginning of his leap into space. The umbrella was fully extended, looking like a black mushroom

above his head. The next moment, the mushroom flew up into an upside-down collapsed shape and Bobby crashed to the ground, with his audience appreciating how funny the whole episode was. We laughed until we cried, then realized that Bobby wasn't getting up to take his well-earned bow. He wasn't laughing, but crying in pain, and since the whole performance had happened right outside Dad's window, it took only a moment for that window to open and Dad's head to stick out. His brown hair was tousled, his brown eyes were squinty at the shock of daylight, and his brown mustache under his large nose seemed to be alive, as he roared, "What's going on down there?!"

When he noticed Bobby lying on the ground in obvious pain, his head disappeared back into the window opening. He hadn't waited for an answer to his question and that worried us, when suddenly he appeared at the backdoor, again in his grey long underwear. My mom had been in the basement washing clothes when she noticed the commotion outside the basement window, and with that maternal instinct, knew something was wrong, and she came running. Just then, Bobby slowly brought himself to his feet, with the fresh tears staining his dirty face, as he proudly presented his final trick to his larger audience. His arm looked just like a snake! A crooked snake! It was broken in three places, and even though he was in pain, he was amazed at his accomplishment.

My dad hurriedly got dressed and my parents rushed Bobby to the hospital. His arm was set and a white cast was put on it, which he had to have on for the rest of the spring and part of the summer. Of course, when he returned from Our Lady of Victory Hospital, he had a new sense of wisdom about him, a new knowledge of that unknown, mysterious place of medical miracles. He and I now had a special bond; he got a cast from the hospital, and I had gotten stitches. On the other hand, my dad got another big hospital bill and even crankier.

CHAPTER FOUR

That first summer was a hot one, so we went swimming every chance we could in Lake Erie, our own private pool. That is, all of us except Bobby, whose cast made him miserable. Everyone had signed it, so it was no longer a clean white, but a mishmash of messages. Sometimes we would take fishing rods along and fish with Bobby from the shore, just to keep him company. One day, we all had our rods in the water, but the fish just weren't biting. Eventually, Donny got fed up with the wait. With his blond hair blowing in the breeze, he put his little rod down and walked into the water, fully clothed in a yellow shirt and shorts. Going in up to his chest, he stood there, carefully examining the smooth surface, when suddenly he pounced on his target. Then he turned and walked back to shore, proudly carrying a six-inch long fish in his hands. After showing it off to all on shore, he went back into the water and let it loose. The fish quickly swam away, glad to be back in his own element, never the wiser of the important role he had played in Donny's status as a fisherman.

That first summer we experienced another event for the first time: the daily arrival of an ice cream truck. Oh, it was wondrous to think of the daily possibilities! Would we buy a Creamsicle, or Fudgesicle, or Popsicle or Klondike? Or maybe an ice cream sandwich! To hear the sound of that song, "My Hat, It Has Three Corners," made us salivate before the truck came into view.

There was only one problem. With six children, it was just too expensive for my parents to buy us ice cream daily. My mom, the frugal one, made the decision after the first time she bought for all of us. As we all sat around on the large front porch and enjoyed eating the best food ever invented, she finished her Klondike, then wiped her mouth with a napkin. She stood up and gathered her soft brown hair back behind her ear where a comb held it in place, behind each ear. Her hazel eyes looked at her children in a serious way and we all took notice, even though we were trying to eat our treats as neatly as possible.

"Children," she said. "I'm sorry, but we can't afford to do this too often. It's too expensive. So we'll look forward to buying from the ice cream truck on payday. Please don't bother me begging for money any other day. We can't afford it."

Payday! Why that was once every two weeks! That wonderful truck, filled with delicious ice cream, was going to drive slowly past our house every single day, and we were expected to buy that delicious ice cream only once every two weeks! Something had to be done about this situation, and fast. We each had to figure out our own methods to make money every day. For the first time, we weren't a group, a team, or even siblings … but business competitors, with only twenty-three hours to figure out a business plan to acquire a daily fortune, in order to become regular customers of the ice cream truck.

Having a pretty good business head on my shoulders at such a young age, I was proud of my plan. It involved the only brother who was younger than me: Donny. He was seventeen months younger and still at that adorable stage, with chunky cheeks, yellow-white hair and dimples on his knees. With his big blue eyes always looking for excitement, I knew he'd go along with my plan.

The next morning, I picked out the outfit that he looked the cutest in: his yellow shirt and shorts. Remember his fishing outfit? After breakfast I figured I'd better work quickly, while he was still clean. Getting our old wagon from the backyard, we started on our quest.

Some new houses had been built the year before, just around the corner from our place. When we walked over to the area, I told Donny to climb into the wagon. Then I pulled him to the side door of the first house. After I rang the doorbell, a nice lady came to the door. Even though I had some front teeth missing, I put on my sweetest smile, as I asked her if she would like to buy a cute little boy for only twenty-five cents. She laughed and said no, she didn't need any little boys, but she told me to wait a minute. Then she disappeared into the house, returning a few seconds later. She said I could keep the little boy, but please take this, and she placed a quarter in my hand. Twenty-five cents!

WOW! My plan worked! So that neighborhood became our territory for earning ice cream money that summer. The next summer, when Donny was bigger, he protested getting into the wagon to be sold, so we would pick pretty flowers from one house and sell them to another. That worked fairly well too, and so we earned our own ice cream treat almost daily. The sound of that truck approaching was the promise of happiness to us. But my dad was not happy, for every single day that jingle, "My Hat, It Has Three Corners," would wake him, and he said that someday he was going to give that hat four corners!

CHAPTER FIVE

Since Donny was the youngest, our mom would occasionally dress him in cute outfits, especially when we were expecting company. Once she dressed me in a pretty blue sun-dress with tiny pink ponies bordering the skirt. Then she dressed Donny in a white sailor-suit, hat and all. We asked if we could go outside to wait for the visitor's arrival while she got herself ready. She said, "Yes, but stay clean!"

In that day in rural areas, modern sanitation improvements, such as buried sewer pipes, were a hope for a distant future. Septic systems were the norm, and runoff ditches bordered every country road. On hot days, after a rain, the sewage and rain runoff co-mingled in those ditches, and in high humidity the stench rose from those areas like a mist over a swamp.

When Donny and I went outside that day, a soft rain had stopped about an hour before and the mist was rising, as was our curiosity to get closer to this natural phenomenon. We walked alongside the ditch, peering into the depths of the moving black water, when suddenly, Donny slipped and fell in, fully submerged for a moment! I screamed and everyone came running: our mom with half her hair still in curlers, and our dad in his summer pajamas. Donny was crying … a pretty good tactic to get some sympathy, at least from Mom, as Dad hollered, "How many times have I told you kids not to go near the ditch?! You could have drowned, Donny!"

Mom scooped him out of the slimy water and set him on the grass. It was amazing ... two big blue eyes shining out of a totally black, smelly creature! The crisp white sailor-suit was unrecognizable, covered completely in black sewage!

As the visitor arrived, my mother was busy washing Donny with a hose on the side of the house, while Dad ran inside, back to his bedroom, to try to get back to sleep. The visitor thought it was very exciting, and realizing that my mom had her hands full with a major kid clean-up, graciously decided to leave and schedule her visit for another time. Before she left, though, she did compliment me on my pretty dress, so the day wasn't a total washout ... only for Donny, that is. As for his sailor's hat, it was never found. A few days later, after returning from fishing, Ralph swore he saw a fish in Lake Erie wearing a sailor's hat!

CHAPTER SIX

Soon after Donny's ditch-diving, we were playing in the dining room, when a pesky fly kept bothering us. Donny didn't really care, but I hated flies, especially this one, and I decided we had a mission … to kill this obnoxious fly. I tried to get him with a flyswatter when he landed on the table, but he was too quick for me. Next, he landed on the mahogany buffet, and again I smacked at him, only to have him buzz around as though taunting me. When he landed on the beautiful crystal chandelier hanging over the shiny mahogany table, I could no longer reach him with the flyswatter. The fly seemed to know he had outsmarted me and he continued to rest on the chandelier, when I had an idea as to how we could reach it. I ran to the pantry, off the country kitchen, and brought back the perfect long weapon to kill that fly: a broom! Handing that broom to Donny, I gave him instructions on what to do next, and he followed my directions perfectly.

Placing that upside-down broom over his right shoulder as though it were a bat, he took a swing at that filthy fly and hit a home run. Or I should say, as the crystal chandelier came crashing down to the table, the home run became a run from the home as we both hightailed it out of there! Just then, Dad came running down the stairs in his pajamas, yelling, "What was that crash?!"

Dad was upset at being shocked out of his sleep, and he was furious when he saw the smashed chandelier, knowing it would cost quite a bit of money to replace it. He complained loudly, but Mom, ever the protector, explained what had happened, after we came out of hiding and explained it to her. She said, "It was an accident, Verne. They didn't mean any harm. They were just trying to kill a fly. You know how much I hate flies. They thought they were doing me a favor, Dear."

When Mom talked like that, in soothing tones, Dad couldn't stay mad for long. But he did say, under his breath, as he went back upstairs to bed, "Accident, my eye! How can a broom bashing into an antique crystal chandelier be an accident?!"

Mom turned on the radio to some mellow music to help him get back to sleep, as she hummed along and cleaned up the mess. In our minds, Mom was great and Dad was mean and getting meaner by the day. But then payday would finally arrive and everyone seemed happy again, especially as we sat around the front porch eating our delicious ice cream, as Mom would tell stories about her childhood. We loved the long, lazy days of summer, even though the older boys had to help out, sometimes. But play was usually the main event.

CHAPTER SEVEN

Near the end of one summer, when the neighboring farm had corn stalks reaching for the sky, we decided to play hide-and-seek. All five of my brothers hid and I was to find them, one by one. Only it never happened that way. I didn't find a single one, but they all found me, instead, as I let out a piercing scream. What had made me scream? Well, I was running through the jungle of corn stalks, when suddenly I ran smack into the middle of a perfect spider web stretched between two corn stalks, exactly at my eye level. At the last moment, I came to an abrupt stop as the huge spider web shook an inch away from my face, and the yellow and black spider held on for the ride of his life! And then I screamed. That's when all my brothers came out of hiding to find me, standing terrified and paralyzed with fear.

But what had scared me only fascinated my brothers. None of us had ever seen such a huge, or colorful spider, and they checked it out thoroughly. Then Ralph, the oldest, decided to turn the spider into a target, as he pulled his slingshot from the back pocket of his blue jeans. He picked up some rocks, as we all stood back. Then he took careful aim, pulled back the thick rubber band and let loose. Tall and lanky with a blond cowlick standing at attention, his blue eyes looking huge behind his thick glasses, and his slightly bucked teeth peering out an inch below his scrunched up nose, he was the picture of intensity. The first rock hit to the right side of the web and shook the spider, again. Then the next shot was a bull's eye, or rather a spider's back, as Ralph hit it and knocked it flying from the web.

Just then, Dad came running through the corn and asked what the screaming had been about. As I tried to explain about running into the spectacular spider with my face, he looked around and said, "I don't see any huge spider. Now tell me what really happened!"

He didn't believe me and my proof was blown to bits. Then my wonderful brothers came to my rescue again and verified what had happened. When they told how Ralph had shot it to kingdom come with his slingshot, my dad seemed disappointed. I think he wanted to see such an amazing spider as we described. In a way, I think we were all disappointed that it was no longer there, minding its own business, hanging between two tall stalks loaded with ripe corn, a beautifully designed yellow and black creation in the middle of its own work of art, its web. If only I hadn't run into it and had it shake back and forth right in my face, then I would not have screamed, and it would still be alive. Now I started crying softly, because I felt sorry for the poor spider, and I felt sad that my dad didn't get to share in seeing it. Dad made some gruff statement to Ralph to be careful with that slingshot, that someone could get hurt, even though we all knew someone already had. Then Dad made his way out of the cornfield and back to the house. We knew he would try to get back to sleep, and we hoped that he could.

CHAPTER EIGHT

As that summer was coming to an end, we all tried to be outside as much as possible. One day, while Mom was hanging clothes on the clothesline in the backyard, and I was playing alone with my little dishes on the front porch, I heard the sound of an engine up in the sky. Running off the porch to get a better view, I noticed an old man stopped in front of our house, also looking up at the sound in the sky. It was a small airplane flying low, right over our house, and it made a motion of tipping its wings to both sides. Then I noticed something familiar, looking out the window of the plane … a boy with straight light-brown hair and glasses. What I was witnessing was so exciting, I could hardly believe it. My brother Bobby was in an actual airplane, flying in the sky and waving! At that time, none of us, including my parents, had ever flown in a plane. The fact that Bobby broke the bonds of earth first made me laugh with joy. And filled with pride, I said to the old man standing nearby, laughing with me, "That's my brother Bobby flying in that airplane! He waved at me!"

"Not only did he wave at you," the old man said with a raspy chuckle, "the plane also waved when it tipped its wings!"

"Oh, I didn't know that!" I answered, happy that he had shared that knowledge with me. Since we had also shared the whole airplane sighting, I felt good manners required something more, so I asked him if he would like a cup of my make-believe tea.

"I would enjoy that tremendously as I am surely parched after walking in all this heat," he responded, again in the raspy voice.

So I led him up the four steps to the front porch and proceeded to pour him a drink from my teapot, which was painted pink. What I pretended was tea was actually water, and I filled a cup and offered it to him. He drank it down

in one gulp and asked if he may have another. With his snowy-white hair, his twinkling blue eyes, and his slightly bent, thin, frail body bearing the burden of many years, he radiated a gentleness and a kindness of spirit. His gnarled fingers held the teacup as though it were the finest china. And boy, was he ever thirsty! He drank cup after cup of my make-believe tea. After he seemed to be satisfied, I asked him his name and he answered, "Grandpa."

Wow! That was a great name, because my two grandpas were far away in Ohio, so I could really use another grandpa. We were having the nicest conversation, with him pointing to different flowers and trees in my yard and telling me their names, when suddenly, a police car pulled up in front of my house and then drove into the driveway. This day was getting more interesting by the moment, as far as I was concerned. First, the airplane with Bobby in it waving, then my new friend sharing my tea party, and now a police car!

After the police car came to a stop, an extremely handsome policeman opened the car door and got out. As he approached the front porch, he put his police hat on his thick, wavy brown hair and walked up the steps. Never had I seen a face like his before. His dark brown eyes were framed in long black lashes, and his chiseled tan face had a dimple right in the middle of his chin. When he spoke, his voice had a deep tone that made me suddenly feel shy.

"Good afternoon," he said, pleasantly, and Grandpa and I sounded like a duet as one raspy voice and one high child's voice together responded, "Good afternoon."

But what the handsome policeman said next totally changed my view of him. "Come on, Pops. It's time to go back to the home."

The home! Grandpa was already at the home. My home! And I wanted him to stay! So I angrily said, "No! You can't take my grandpa!" I felt I was defending some unknown principle of friendship and kinship.

When the policeman realized I was going to defend my rights to keep my new friend, he knew he had a battle on his hands, and he would need to call in reinforcements ... meaning my parents. So he rang the doorbell, loud and clear. Since I knew my mom was in the backyard, I felt safe in my position. Again, he pressed on the doorbell, only this time he kept his finger on that button for what seemed like forever. Then a sound came from inside the house. Oh no! He had woken my dad! I decided it was time to surrender and I did it in the age-old way of women: I cried. Oh, did I ever cry! My heart was breaking, and I wanted everyone to know.

Then my dad appeared at the door, and took in the situation with one sweeping glance. There we stood, one little red-haired girl sobbing, one handsome policeman, who could contend with the most villainous criminal, but not a sobbing child, and one elderly gentleman, looking confused.

"What's going on here?!" he asked in an angry loud voice, as we all started explaining, simultaneously.

"One at a time," my dad ordered, and even though his dark brown hair was tousled from sleep and he was in his light cotton burgundy pajamas, he still emitted a sense of strength, dignity, and command.

The policeman went first, explaining that the nursing home one mile up the road had reported a missing person, an elderly man who looked just like the man on the porch. Then the officer reached into his pocket, pulled out a folded paper and opened it. Sure enough, there was a picture of my new grandpa!

That picture stopped my crying, but I was still sniffling as I said, "Daddy, this is my new grandpa and we're having a tea party. Can't I keep him?"

Looking at the old man, my father started to have the hint of a smile on his face as he said, "So, what's your story?"

As far as the old man could tell, he wasn't too sure of his story, so he said, "I'm at a tea party with her. May I have another cup of tea, please?"

The look that the policeman and my father exchanged spoke volumes, but all my dad said was, "Sure, you can have more tea. Betty Jean, please pour the nice man some more tea."

What he didn't know was that I was all out of my make-believe tea. Grandpa and I had already finished the entire teapot. "But, Daddy, there is no more! It's all gone!"

Then my dad did a strange thing. He told us to wait a minute and he went into the house. A few moments later, he returned with the pitcher of lemonade, which my mother made daily, in one hand, and a plate of Fig Newton cookies in the other hand.

As the policeman held the door for him, I sensed something special was happening. The policeman removed his hat and placed it on the wide porch railing, as my dad poured cold lemonade into four teacups. Then Grandpa and I sat on the green glider, and the policeman and my dad, in his pajamas, sat on two Adirondack chairs. Dad passed around the plate of cookies, and as we drank lemonade and ate Fig Newtons, I realized this turned out to be my best tea party of all time! Then my mom came around the side of the house and noticed the police car in the driveway, so she hurried to the front of the house to see what was wrong. When she took in the scene on the porch, she was astonished, and her face had a look of wonder … like, "I wonder what in the world is going on here!"

Nothing was wrong; everything was absolutely right, and she sensed it. And with the way my parents had of sometimes communicating without speaking, my dad gave her a look that said, "I'll explain everything later," as he said, "Have a cookie, Honey!"

When it was finally time to say good-bye to my new friends, I shook hands with the police officer, and I gave Grandpa a big hug. We all had smiles on our faces, but tears in our eyes, as the handsome nice policeman escorted the dignified, elderly gentleman to the police car. As they drove away, both waving farewell, I gained a nugget of wisdom that day: friends come in all shapes, clothes, and ages.

A few minutes later, Bobby showed up full of excitement and questions: "Did you see me flying in an airplane? We waved at you with our hands and with the wings! Did you see?! And how come a police car was here?!" His words spilled out like make-believe tea pouring into a cup.

When my parents recognized that Bobby had actually flown in an airplane, they acted upset, saying he must never do anything like that again without their permission.

"It's too dangerous!" my mom said, as Dad added, "You could have been killed!"

Then Bobby pulled out a little card from his pants pocket and proudly presented his official co-pilot's license, with even his name on it! That impressed the entire family, and when all my other brothers returned home that day, they were all a little envious of Bobby and me. We had both had unique experiences that helped us grow: Bobby gained courage, and I gained wisdom and compassion.

A few days later, my mom called the nursing home to learn how my friend was doing, and she was told he had passed away the day after we had met him. The nurse said he had told the other residents he felt the end was near, and he wanted one more walk. So at the age of ninety-two, he had walked nearly one mile to our home and right into my tea party. How privileged I felt to have met him. I'll never forget my special, hand-picked grandpa. Meeting him seemed to have softened up my dad for a while, too. It didn't last for long, though.

CHAPTER NINE

That summer, a housing development was being built a couple of blocks away. Some farmland had been cleared and cute Cape Cod houses were constructed as my brothers and I had ringside seats, watching every step of the building process. We enjoyed the organized way each section was made. First, the steam shovel excavated the huge hole for the basement. Then the cement blocks were put up, one by one, on the sides of the hole, forming the basement walls and the foundation for the house. Next, the carpenters hammered nails into the lumber and built the structure. Then the roofers put the shingles on, and that's as far as we could watch. Everything else was done inside, away from our curious eyes.

But Bobby, ever the friendly, helpful boy, made friends with some of the builders and before we knew it, he was doing little odd jobs for the workers: fetching a hammer, helping to clean up, bringing their coffee to them. When the first house was completed, he came home with a self-confidence and pride that was wonderful to see. Then he pulled a small card from his pants and proudly displayed it. There it was in writing with his name and the date all formally stating that Bobby was now an honorary member of a carpenter's union! We could not believe it! Bobby had two cards, a co-pilot and a carpenter, and the rest of us had none … Zero … Zilch! But we were happy for him. (Then I finally received a card and felt special, too. I had a card to carry. How proud I was of my library card!)

After the first house was completed and the "For Sale" sign was placed in the front yard, the builders went down the street a bit and started building the next home. So that left the first house as an object of curiosity. What did the

inside look like, we wondered. Living in an old farm house made us wonder what a new, modern house would have that would be so different from ours.

From the first street of houses that had been completed the previous year, were two brothers whose reputations for being rascals were well-known. Their parents were very nice, and their dad was our milkman, so I thought I'd give the boys a chance and be friends. If anyone knew how to get along with boys, I was that person. Or so I thought.

But one day the brothers came over to play in our yard, and within five minutes were in a fight with my brothers. As they turned to leave, yelling curse words we were hearing for the first time, one of them bent down and picked up a rock. Now I wasn't even a participant in the argument, and I was just innocently standing there, when all of a sudden, he threw that rock directly at me and hit me in my forehead! Then they ran for dear life, as my brothers chased them and I cried loudly in pain, as blood gushed out of my head and poured down my face. My brothers turned around and realized their dilemma: continue to chase the aggressors or come to the aid of the victim, their little sister. They came running back to help me and calm me, but even they were scared, because there sure was a lot of blood on me.

When they took me back to the house, my mom became very upset, which woke up my dad, who took one look at me and said they'd better take me to the hospital. Not again! Even though I was beginning to feel weak, I put up a fight. I didn't want to go to the hospital again, and get a shot or stitches. My mother held a clean dishtowel to my forehead, and in a little while the bleeding stopped. So she made a deal with me: if I would let her wash my wound and put peroxide on it, then maybe I would not have to go to the hospital. Washing and peroxide seemed better than the shots and stitches, so I agreed. When the wound was cleaned and medicated, she put a large bandage over it. It would eventually heal nicely, but I would always have a scar … and wear bangs.

Since my dad was awake now, he became the inquisitor, getting the entire story from my brothers and learning that I had been an innocent bystander. After he had all the facts, he turned to me and said in a serious voice: "Betty Jean, don't you ever go near those two boys again! They're bad and they'll only hurt you. Do you hear me?"

"Yes, Daddy," I meekly replied.

Oh, if only I had listened to him … if only I had obeyed my dad, what happened right before Christmas vacation would never have happened!

CHAPTER TEN

Autumn had arrived, which meant we were all back at school during the week. With all of us having homework to do, that left only the weekends for new adventures. And guess who was in my class … Billy Bateman, the older bad brother that my dad had warned me to never go near! But he was in my class, and though I stayed away from him, I watched him out of the corner of my eye. He often got into fights with other boys on the playground at recess, and he basically ignored the girls, which was fine with me. That all changed one weekend.

It was early December, and I had heard the rumor that the new house had been sold, so I decided to walk over there, by myself, to see if the new family had moved in yet, and more importantly, if they had any kids my age, preferably a girl. As I approached the driveway, I didn't see any sign of activity; no family had moved in yet. In my curiosity to get a better look, just to make sure the home was still vacant, I walked down the driveway, when suddenly, from behind the house, out walked Billy Bateman!

Never expecting to see him there, I was shocked, and my face must have shown it. But he did something totally unexpected; he acted all nice and friendly, like I was just the person he was hoping to see.

"Hi, Betty Jean," he greeted me, happily. "What are you doing here?"

"I wanted to see if a family moved in yet," I responded bravely, putting aside all caution and ignoring my father's warning in what happened next.

"Do you want to see the inside of the house?!" Billy asked, excitedly. "The doors are locked, but I know a special way we can get into the house and look around, and no one will ever know. Come on, it'll be fun!" he urged persuasively.

Getting caught up in the excitement of the moment, I thought what harm could possibly happen if two curious kids wanted to take a tour of the empty new house. So I agreed to his plan.

"Sure, that'll be fun!" I said. "Only, how are we going to get in if all the doors are locked?" I asked.

"Just follow me," he answered, as he led the way up four steps to a small side porch.

Then he pointed at something I had never seen before, on the side of the house. It was a miniature square door cut right into the house, and as he unlocked the door by turning a latch, he explained what it was.

"This is something the new, modern houses have," he said, proud of his knowing something I didn't know. "It's a special compartment for my dad to put the bottles of milk, when he delivers them before the people who live here are even awake. They'll leave him a note in this compartment, telling him how much milk to leave, and once a week, they'll leave the payment for the milk in an envelope, after he leaves a bill. That way, he never has to bother anyone, knocking at doors or ringing doorbells so early in the morning. He'll put the milk inside and the people will open the small door that's inside, and remove the milk and put it into their refrigerators. Isn't this a great invention?" he asked.

"Oh yes!" I answered, and I was really impressed with both the modern invention and his knowledge of it.

Then he put his entire arm through, and the inner door hanging from the top hinges swung open. He was right! We could see the inside of the house, as he further explained: "All we have to do is climb through both doors and then we'll be in. Then we could look all through the house before anyone else sees it. And no one will ever know!"

His excitement was catching, and so was his logic. As he started to put his upper body into the compartment, he suddenly stopped and exclaimed with a laugh, "Where are my manners?! Ladies first!" as he stood aside, holding the outer door opened for me to go through first.

So I climbed through that milk compartment head first, and Billy Bateman was ever so polite as he pushed my body through, until I landed inside the new kitchen, falling out of the milk compartment a couple of feet to the floor. I was so excited to be inside the vacant house as I stood up and looked around, saying to Billy, whose head was poking through the inner door, "Oh, isn't this pretty?! Wow, what a nice kitchen!"

Suddenly, Billy pulled his head back out of the compartment and I heard a slamming sound, followed by another strange sound, that of the turning of a lock. Then I heard evil laughter, first on the porch, but then getting fainter. I reached through the compartment to try to push the outer door open, but it wouldn't move.

The house was locked from the outside. Billy Bateman had locked me into an empty house! That's when my dad's words echoed in my mind: "Betty Jean, don't you ever go near those two boys again! They're bad and they'll only hurt you!"

Oh no, I thought. Why didn't I listen to him? My dad was right, and I didn't obey him. Now I was in trouble and I had to figure a way to get out of that house!

Looking around the kitchen, I immediately noticed how beautiful it was. There were white shiny counters all along two walls, with soft peach colored wooden cabinets above and below the counters. The floor was a pretty brown design that matched the trim around the cabinets. There was a built-in white refrigerator and some other thing which I had never seen before: an automatic dishwasher, it said on the door! Well, we had seven dishwashers at my house, I thought, including my mom, but the only thing automatic was that my brothers automatically argued every night as to whose turn it was to do the dishes!

When I thought of that, I softly laughed to myself and I figured, I might as well have my tour of the house, since I was in there. So I went from room to room, thinking how lucky the family was who would eventually move into that beautiful home. The large living room had a fireplace on one wall, and there were three bedrooms and two bathrooms. I searched the entire first and second floors and then decided I'd better find a way out of that house, because I noticed through the upstairs window that the sun was setting. As I stood at the window watching the beautiful colors of sunset, it dawned on me that it was going to be dark soon!

Hurrying down the stairs, I ran to the backdoor, but it was locked with a strange lock, and I couldn't unlock the door. So I went to the front door, and it also had that kind of lock! Then I started to panic! What if I could never get out! I opened the refrigerator door, but it was empty and not even cold. No food … I was going to starve to death! Even though it was a mild day, the house was cold, since it was December. As it turned colder I was going to freeze to death! The window locks were too high for me to reach, but darkness was setting in quickly … if I didn't get home soon, my dad was going to kill me! Well, maybe not actually "kill" me, but punish me so that I wished I was dead! What could I do?! I sat on the floor and I cried for a while, cursing Billy Bateman for getting me into this situation. Then I realized I had to take the blame: I didn't have to listen to him … I could have listened to my dad.

My imagination started playing tricks on me as the house got darker. When a car would drive down the street, reflections on the walls would look strange and I started to hear noises! Then I felt sorry for myself and started sobbing. I felt sorry for my family when they all would realize I was gone forever. I even felt sorry for the new family who would move into their wonderful new home and find my dead body. That's when I snapped out of my misery and decided I had to take action! Sure, I couldn't reach the windows on the first floor; but what if I tried to climb to the window above the kitchen sink and counter, I thought.

The streetlight had gone on at the corner and was shining through the window in the kitchen. I opened a cabinet door, but I couldn't reach to hoist myself up to the counter. Then I felt the knobs and pulled on one. A drawer came out! That's when I found my solution to that window above the sink: I pulled the drawers out, the bottom one further and the higher ones less, and I climbed up the drawers like a ladder.

When I reached the top, I crawled onto the counter and over to the window. Then I prayed: "Dear God, help me to get out of this house. I promise I'll listen to my dad from now on, and I'll never trust Billy Bateman or bad people again. Please, God, help me!"

Just then I noticed a person walking around the corner. It was an older neighbor girl, Patty Anderson, a friend of my brother David. I started screaming and pounding on the window. She suddenly stopped and looked around with a frown on her face, lit up by the streetlight. Screaming louder and pounding frantically, I must have frightened her. She looked right at the window, then she approached the house, cautiously. When she finally got to the window and recognized me, she yelled from down below, "What are you doing in that house, Betty Jean?! How did you get in there?!"

Yelling back, almost hysterical now, I told her how Billy Bateman had locked me in and run away. I told her to unlatch the little door on the side porch, so that I could get out. Then I climbed down my drawer ladder and went over to the special milk compartment. When I opened the inner door, Patty had already unlocked and opened the outer door, and again I climbed through, head first. Patty pulled me out and then started hollering at me, as I tried to explain about Billy Bateman's promise of a secret house tour. "I can't believe you listened to him!" she said, angrily. "Don't you know he's a liar, and a thief, and if I hadn't come along and the new people aren't moving in for a couple of weeks yet, he would be a murderer, because you could have died in there all alone! I'm telling your parents what happened! Now let's go!" she ordered, as she took me home, holding my hand and hollering at me the whole way. And I deserved it. But after that, I always considered Patty Anderson as an angel from God … an angry angel.

When we arrived home, my family was upset, especially my dad. My mom had to hold him back from going over to Billy Bateman's house and strangling him with his bare hands, after Patty explained what had happened to me. My mom hugged me fiercely as I sobbed. Eventually, my sobs subsided and my stomach growled. Even though I had missed supper, my mom set a delicious bowl of homemade vegetable soup out for me and it was the best soup I had ever tasted!

All my brothers sat around the table watching me eat, and asking so many questions, I felt like I was on a quiz show. Then I took a nice, hot bath and climbed into my bed with such a feeling of gladness. I was so happy to be home in my warm bed, surrounded by the warm love of my wonderful family, including all five of my brothers, who were good and kind, not bad like Billy and Davey Bateman. That night, I thanked God for saving me and for giving me such a loving family. I prayed for Patty Anderson to be blessed. And I prayed for Billy Bateman to change into a good person. I could always hope, couldn't I?

The next time the milkman came, my parents angrily confronted him with what his sons had done to me, especially Billy. Mr. Bateman apologized and cried. He said he didn't know why they were doing bad things, and he promised he would discipline them more in the future. I felt sorry for Mr. Bateman. He was a nice man. But I never went near his sons again.

A couple of weeks later, right before Christmas, two great things happened: Buffalo got a really deep snow, and I got my first best friend. Michaelene Kushner moved into the new house I had been locked in, and she was the same age as I was. Finally, a girl for a friend! When she wanted to show me around her new home, it looked even better with furniture and curtains and a family. Another secret prayer had been answered.

~~~~

At home, Dad made a new rule: everyone had to be home before dark, or at least the younger kids. Anyone disobeying that rule had to go to bed without supper. Of course, Bobby ended up hungry many a night, given his adventurous spirit. I did what I could for him: I would make a peanut butter and jelly sandwich, wrap it in wax paper, stick it in my jean's pocket, with an apple in the other pocket, and sneak upstairs to his room. He would be so happy to see me and the sandwich. Dad would yell from downstairs, "Betty Jean, what are you doing?!"

"Nothing, Daddy, just visiting Bobby," I would respond.

"Well, Bobby is being punished and doesn't need any visitors, so you get downstairs now, you hear?!" he would explode.

So I would hurry back down the stairs with empty pockets and a full heart of "mission accomplished."

CHAPTER ELEVEN

The night before Christmas finally arrived and Donny, Bobby and I were so excited for the night to pass, that we were ready for bed at seven o'clock. Each of us had sat on Santa's lap at the department store in downtown Buffalo, and we had listed our gift wishes, so we figured, the sooner we went to bed, the sooner Santa would come and fulfill those wishes. But my mother and father and older brothers didn't want us going to sleep too early or we would wake them up way too early on Christmas morning.

So finally, at nine o'clock on Christmas Eve, after eating a delicious meal topped off with buttered nut kolache, singing Christmas carols, hanging our stockings, and kissing everyone goodnight, we went upstairs, jumped into our beds, said our prayers with Mom, and snuggled under the blankets, waiting for sleep to come. We waited … and waited … and waited. Donny conked out first, but Bobby and I sure were wide awake. The clock on the dresser had numbers that glowed in the dark; those numbers showed it was twelve o'clock midnight!

Sneaking to the top of the stairs, Bobby and I heard all kinds of commotion from the living room below. A floorboard must have squeaked because my brother Ralph came to the bottom of the stairs, looked up and saw me. "Betty Jean, get to bed!" Ralph yelled, alerting everyone to my presence.

Bobby ran back to bed, but a sense of panic made me yell back: "Santa's going to go right over our house and leave us nothing if all of you don't go to bed! How is he supposed to come here with all of you still awake and downstairs near the tree?! I'm telling you, he's going to skip us this year if you all don't get up here and go to bed, too!" I stomped my foot for emphasis, and the sounds of laughter rose from the living room. "Betty Jean!" my dad roared. "Don't make me come up there! Get to sleep now!"

"Now Verne," came my mom's soothing voice. "She's just excited, that's all. I'll go tuck her in again." Then she came up the stairs as I ran and jumped into bed.

When she sat on the side of my bed and caressed my face, she said, softly, "Honey, Santa will come to our home. Don't worry. We're on his later schedule. He's over the Atlantic Ocean right now, because he just finished giving gifts to the children in Russia and Germany, England and Spain, Italy and Ireland, Poland and Romania, Czechoslovakia and Hungary, France and Yugoslavia …" The list went on and on, and I felt myself getting drowsy. She got up and tiptoed out of my bedroom.

Oh no! I don't know those children from those other places, but I want to make sure our place is ready for Santa, I thought to myself as I snuck out of bed again and went to the window. It was snowing, so that was good for Santa to land on the roof. I saw a red light in the distance and watched it move through the sky. That surely must be Rudolf, the red-nosed reindeer that we sang about in school. As I followed the red light moving slowly through the gently falling snow, I hoped Santa went to Michaelene's house first, because my mom and dad and three older brothers were still awake downstairs. That was my last thought, as I fell asleep on the floor, under the window, and at the foot of the bed.

When I woke up the next morning, I was lying on the floor and someone had covered me with a blanket. Wondering what I was doing sleeping on the floor, I looked around the room from this vantage point. Boy, everything sure was neat and clean: under the bed was spotless and shoes were lined up. Then I remembered: Mom had been cleaning, and baking and cooking all week for Christmas. And this was Christmas!

Getting up off the floor, I ran to wake Bobby and Donny and we all hurried down the stairs, filled with the excitement known to children around the world on one magical morning of the year. As we tore into the wrapping paper covering our presents, our excitement rose, as did our voices, and before we knew it, the whole family was awake and joined us around the tree, as Mom turned the radio to the sounds of Christmas carols, and we exposed each treasure.

For Donny, there was a gas station and cars and trucks. For Bobby, there was a wagon and a new fishing rod, a sled, and a wallet for his co-pilot and carpenter cards! And for me, there was a dollhouse, filled with furniture in every room! Wow, just what we wanted! A big gift was still wrapped and the tag said, "To Betty Jean and Donny, Love from Santa." So we tore off the wrapping paper together and looked with amazement at the biggest tricycle we had ever seen! I got on the wonderful vehicle first and went zooming from the living room through the dining room, into the kitchen and back to the living room, with everyone cheering me on with laughing voices. Then I came to an abrupt stop, climbed off, and presented it to Donny for his test-drive.

What fun we had that Christmas morning, playing and eating and playing some more. After a while, Dad said he was going back to bed, and something about Santa having a rough night assembling toys, so would we keep the noise level down, please. Since Santa had also brought us other gifts, like games and paint sets, we decided to play quietly with those things until later, after Dad's nap. It was our Christmas gift to him.

CHAPTER TWELVE

When spring finally arrived, we all had had our quota of snow and were glad to see it melt, exposing the emerging buds on all the bushes and trees. My mom especially couldn't wait for the return of green to our world. She cut some short branches from a tree and put them into a vase in the middle of the dining room table. They were called "pussy willows" she said, and we all liked watching them bloom.

As the weather grew warmer, we all played outside more, even though my parents had treated the family to the purchase of something special: a brand new television. It seemed like my dad was the one who enjoyed watching it the most, and many days he fell asleep on the couch, while the television was on. He loved seeing a boxing show, a circus show and Milton Berle's show. The programming for children did not impress my brothers or me: Howdy Doody, and Kukla, Fran and Ollie. Personally, I thought both shows were stupid, silly and ridiculous, and I'd rather read a good story and then go outside and re-enact that story with Michaelene and Donny.

One warm spring day, we had visitors. My parents had volunteered to babysit two children whose father worked with my dad. Their parents had to attend a funeral, so basically, Donny and I had special-order playmates that entire day, a boy and a girl. We were all getting along pretty well, when my mom came out and told Donny and me to play a quieter game, so that we didn't wake our dad. After chastising us, she turned to the two strangers and said, "I hope you're enjoying your visit with us," in her nicest voice.

Both children agreed that they were having fun and then something weird happened: they gave Donny and me a look that seemed to say, "Your mother likes us better than she likes you."

Oh yeah, I thought. Well, we'll show you how nice our mom is … That's when I borrowed a page from the Billy Bateman book of bad behavior. Whispering to Donny what I had in mind, I led the way to the backyard and to my mom's clothes props. When the kids asked what I was going to do with two clothes props, I told them Donny and I were going to play a game called "Stop the Traffic." Then we walked around to the front yard and to the main road beyond our bushes. Just then the girl asked, "Can we play, too?" and the boy said, "Yes, can we play, too?"

"Well, yes, you can both have the first turn, but you've got to do the game right," I said. Then I instructed each one to hold a clothes prop in the center and to stand in the middle of each lane. I told them that whoever stopped the most cars was the winner, and they could hardly wait to start the game. They both waited for a few cars to pass. Then they made their move into the road.

As this particular road was the main highway to Buffalo and to Niagara Falls, within a few minutes the game was nearly over, since both lanes were filled with stopped cars, all honking their horns. The racket woke up my dad and he and my mom came running out of the house, looking in amazement at the traffic jam in front of our home. Then they saw the cause of it, and each went into the road and grabbed the clothes props with one hand and the two children with another hand. As soon as they had cleared the street and cars were again moving slowly past, people were yelling things out the windows of their vehicles.

"Why don't you spank those kids and teach them right from wrong before they get killed?!" one man yelled.

As my parents brought both children back into our yard, they were hollering at them, and the kids were crying loudly. From our hiding place behind a lilac bush, Donny and I felt vindicated and then suddenly I felt my jealousy evaporate. What a terrible thing I had done, getting those children into trouble just because I had been jealous of how nice my mom and dad were treating them … I didn't like how I felt, this new feeling known as "guilt." So for the rest of the afternoon, Donny and I made a special effort to show those two kids a good time. We showed them our orchard in bloom, and we let them each take turns riding our big tricycle. When their parents arrived to take them home, no one mentioned the traffic game, and the day ended well. The strange thing was, Donny and I missed them when they were gone. So for a long time afterward, we would have two pretend friends play also. We named them Jeanie and Jonie, and these imaginary friends were great fun, especially for our older brothers to tease!

CHAPTER THIRTEEN

Wherever we went that summer, Jeanie and Jonie went with us, even to the Buffalo Zoo. Donny and I showed them our favorite animals: mine was the beautiful white polar bear, and Donny liked the gorilla. But the gorilla stared at me as I stood next to my mom. Then his eyes followed me as I walked over to where my dad stood. I was thinking the gorilla was very hairy and wondered if he thought the same about me with my long bangs.

After we returned from the zoo, my mom decided that my brothers resembled the hairy animals a little too much, and therefore they all needed haircuts, since they all still had their winter growth. The hair cutting set she had bought a couple of years before was put to good use again, as she lined up five bushy boys and gave them each a summer cut. When she was done, they all looked different, but good. Of course, they all made fun of each other, pointing and laughing.

As for my own hair, I was getting sick of it being in my eyes all the time. My mom would brush it in the morning and tell me how pretty my red-gold color was, as she braided it and pinned it back. But after a few hours of play, it would fall into my eyes and make me cranky. My five brothers never had to worry about hair falling into their eyes all summer long. It wasn't fair and I decided to do something about it.

After everyone went to bed that night, I quietly sneaked out of my room and into the bathroom, where the night-light was shining dimly. The hair cutting set was in a cupboard and I quickly found what I wanted: the scissors. With it being nearly dark, I really couldn't see what I was doing, so I had to feel my way. Having watched my mom cut hair all evening, I thought I knew how to do it. I grabbed the hair on the top of my head, the hair that was always bothering me, and I cut it pretty close to my scalp. Then I grabbed another clump and cut again. Since it was almost dark, I had to use the touch and feel process of hair cutting. I continued this procedure until I felt it was no longer going to be a problem, always falling into my eyes. After a while, I felt my job was done and I headed back to bed, feeling I had really accomplished my goal: no more hair in my eyes!

The next morning, I woke up to a scream. My mom had walked into my bedroom, taken one look at me and screamed! Geez maneez! What was wrong?! I was a little confused at first, until I heard her say, "What happened to your hair?! Who did that to you?!"

My brothers came running and when they saw me, they started laughing hysterically. "Did one of you do this to her?!" my mom asked, and they all denied knowing anything about my radical, new haircut.

Realizing something must be wrong and that I had to deflect the blame away from myself, I did some quick thinking. Modern psychology would say my defense mechanism kicked in, big time. "What happened, Betty Jean? Who did this to you?" my mom asked again.

Without hesitation, I announced to all, "A gorilla did it. A gorilla came through my window in the night and cut my hair. The gorilla didn't want me to have hair in my eyes like he had, so he cut my hair." I looked at their shocked faces. Then they all burst out laughing! They laughed till tears were rolling down their faces. Then we heard a noise downstairs. Dad was home from work!

"Where is everybody?" he called, and my mom answered that we'd be down in a little while. She told my brothers to go downstairs and keep Dad occupied and don't dare tell him about my hair. Then she took me to the bathroom to try to fix my haircut.

When I saw myself in the mirror, I started to panic. Boy, did I look funny! Not funny good, but funny stupid! My mom picked up the scissors and started damage control. After she was finished, she shampooed my hair, gave me a bath, and styled what was left on my head. To this day, I swear I was the first girl with a pixie cut. The other girls, including Michaelene, wanted to have their hair styled my way. For a summer of fun and adventure, it was perfect. And the next time we went to the zoo, I apologized to the gorilla for having blamed him.

But I felt my dad's disappointment when he first saw my new haircut. He looked at me sadly, and said, "All that beautiful strawberry-blond hair gone …" Then he shook his head.

"Daddy," I tried to explain. "My hair was always in my eyes! People should not have bangs so long that they're in their eyes! It makes a person cranky! There should be a rule: cut kids' bangs short so they don't get cranky from having hair in their eyes. Honest, Daddy, that should be a rule! In fact, grown-up ladies should cut their bangs, too, because they look like old witches when they have bangs in their eyes!" I thought I was defending my view very well, but he said nothing further; he just shook his head and then went to bed.

CHAPTER FOURTEEN

That summer we got a new car, and my parents decided a visit to Ohio would be a nice vacation. The whole family was excited, and I bragged to Michaelene that we were going on a one week vacation to Ohio. After all the preparations were completed, including packing suitcases with our summer clothes and preparing a picnic lunch to be eaten when we were halfway there, we finally started our trip in our shiny, new blue car. I was sitting in between my parents in the front seat, and Donny was sitting on my mom's lap. The four other brothers were crowded into the back seat.

As we started off, Michaelene was waving at us from the side of the road, and I felt a sense of superiority because we were going on vacation. Never having known anyone who had gone on a vacation to another state, I felt proud of my family. We were vacation pioneers.

The plan was to go southwest along Lake Erie until we were in Pennsylvania, and then south to a highway that would take us west to Ohio. But about seven miles into our trip, my four brothers started arguing in the back seat.

"You're hogging all the room!"

"No, you're hogging all the room!"

"Get your elbow out of my side! Mom, he hit me!"

Suddenly, my dad yelled, "Quiet! If I hear one more sound from back there, I'm turning this car around and we're going home!" he threatened.

For about three miles they behaved, but then it started again ... the bickering, the poking, the complaining. If one thing could be said about my dad, it was that he was a man of his word. While the brothers fought, my dad

pulled the shiny, new blue car over to the side of the road. Then, when it was clear to do so, he made a u-turn and headed back toward our house. That was the end of our Ohio vacation!

When we drove back into our driveway, Michaelene came running over to see what was wrong. All my pride went away, and I felt shame as I tried to explain to her about my brothers making my dad mad.

"Gee," she said. "Your dad sure is mean! My dad would never have done that!"

Feeling a sense of loyalty, I defended my dad by saying, "Well, your dad will never know because he has two daughters and no sons to drive him crazy! My dad has five sons, so there!" I felt that explained everything.

For lunch that day, we ate our Ohio picnic food.

CHAPTER FIFTEEN

Even though we never made it back to Ohio for a vacation, that summer turned out to be exciting anyhow, because my Aunt Mary sent my cousin Suzie from Ohio to stay with us all summer. Suzie was my brother David's age, but she was so much fun that she got along with everybody. Natural blond hair and expressive blue eyes were her best features, besides her sparkling, dynamic personality. She had a cute figure at an early age, and when my mom took her shopping for a bathing suit, I went along to help her select the perfect suit.

When she stepped out of the dressing room wearing a bright royal-blue one piece, everyone around stared in appreciation of her beauty. "That's the one!" I exploded, and we all laughed in agreement.

It sure was nice having another female living in our home, but for some reason, which I would not understand for a few years, there were now many more males at our house, also. The word had gotten out to all my brothers' friends about Suzie, and our house became the popular spot that summer. Michaelene and I hung out there occasionally, watching Suzie and the boys all flirt with each other. When we had enough education, we would go to Michaelene's house to play or ride bikes. The older boys would take Suzie swimming or to an amusement park called Crystal Lake. Or they would all go bowling or to a movie. Watching Suzie have so much fun with the boys that summer made me think getting older, and hopefully prettier, might be fun.

Near the end of the summer, Suzie, my brother David, and some of his friends were on the front porch, kidding around. I was there too, and to this

day, I can't believe what I saw happen. David and Suzie were "roughhousing" when suddenly David pushed her and she went crashing right through the large picture window! It made a tremendous noise and I ran over to look at the damage, expecting to see Suzie bleeding profusely. She was lying her back on the living room floor, with shards of glass everywhere! My mom came running into the room with hand to her mouth and her eyes widened in disbelief. The crashing sound had woken my dad and he dashed down the stairs in his summer pajamas, barefooted.

"Verne, be careful! There's glass everywhere! Go get some shoes on! We'll probably have to take her to the hospital, so get your clothes on, too!" my mom said, hurriedly.

I was still on the porch with David, looking through the empty hole and watching for signs of life from Suzie, when suddenly she started to giggle hysterically. "I think I'm okay, Aunt Ann!" she finally managed to say, as my mom carefully made her way over the broken glass to where Suzie lay.

As she moved over Suzie, she reached for both of her hands and pulled her up to a standing position. Then she examined her thoroughly. We always said afterwards that Suzie had a guardian angel. For you see, there was not one single cut on Suzie … not a scratch! It was a miracle to me because I had witnessed the whole thing happen, and it was unbelievable that she escaped unharmed.

My brother David, the one who had pushed her through the plate glass window, didn't escape unharmed, though. Dad punished him, yelled at him, and made him pay for a new window, with the money he earned picking beans in late summer, and delivering newspapers.

When her mom, my Aunt Mary, and her older sister, Barbara, arrived from Ohio to take Suzie back home, the whole neighborhood was sad to see her leaving. I think she left a lot of broken hearts that summer, including mine.

CHAPTER SIXTEEN

Something else happened before the end of the summer that made me realize being a parent was the hardest job, because things happen to children and the parents have to deal with everything, both emotionally and financially. My brother Billy suffered a tragic accident and it saddened my parents deeply.

A neighbor had bought a new invention, a power lawn mower, and the boys of the neighborhood were all trying it. But it had rained earlier in the day and the grass was still wet. Billy was wearing brown leather oxford shoes, and the leather soles were a little slippery on the wet grass. He was pushing the mower down a slight hill, when suddenly his foot slid under the mower!

David came running home, almost in shock, as he told my mom what had happened. She woke my dad who dressed in half a minute, and then they told David to watch us. They ordered us to behave and to listen to David. As they hurried out the front door, we heard the sound of an ambulance nearby. After a few minutes, the siren again started screaming and then the sound faded into the distance. When we asked David to tell us what happened, he started to cry as he told how Billy had cut off his toes! Poor Billy … and poor Mom and Dad …

The next day, my parents returned carrying Billy's shoes, one whole, and one cut into two parts and soaked in dark red blood. They told us the doctors had sewn Billy's toes back onto his foot, and he would be in the hospital for a while. Hopefully, the surgery would be a success, and someday, he would be healed and able to walk again. During those weeks and months, we kids were on our best behavior. We figured our parents had enough to handle.

Seeing the horrible way his shoe was cut in half, it was truly amazing that his foot healed the way it did. After several months, he was able to walk in a perfectly normal manner. The only thing that gave him a little bit of trouble was walking up stairs: his toes didn't bend on the injured foot, so he had to watch that he didn't knock them into the steps. He was careful and managed to do everything he had been able to do before the accident.

But my parents gained a few grey hairs during that awful time. When Billy was able to do the jitterbug, with his brown curly hair bouncing to the rhythm of the music, and his brown eyes sparkling as he sang along to the song, that's when we all knew that he was totally healed, physically and emotionally. How long would it take for my parents to heal was a mystery that time alone would show.

CHAPTER SEVENTEEN

Sometimes I felt that Michaelene was right: my dad was so mean. Many times I wondered if he even liked me. The next spring something happened that showed me he did.

In our large side yard, the many lilac bushes were blooming in glorious splendor: some a light lilac color, some a deeper purple, and some were white. All I knew was that I loved the fragrance all around them, and it would only last a couple of weeks, so I played near them as much as possible. To breathe the beautiful fragrance of the lilac and to see the exquisite beauty of the flower made me feel that heaven must have lilacs.

One day while playing behind the large bushes, I was using a stick to make a mark in the dirt: then I pretended it was a road and I placed stones on my road. They were my cars. In the distance, I heard the sound of sirens, so I pretended one of the stones was a police car. Then the sirens were closer and finally screaming nearby. It sounded like more than one siren, so I pretended another stone was an ambulance. After a while, I decided to color the stones: red for the ambulance and black for the police car. So I got up and walked down the long driveway toward our house to get my crayons.

Just then I noticed a commotion on the road in front of our home. There were two fire trucks, two police cars and an ambulance! And there were my parents, hugging each other and sobbing! What was going on here?! Who hurt my mom and dad?!

Hurrying down the rest of the driveway to where they were standing on the side of the road, I reached them and tugged on my mom's dress, as I said, "Why are you crying, Mommy?"

As she looked down at me, she gasped and then my dad saw me and scooped me up into his arms and hugged me till I thought I wasn't going to be able to breathe anymore! But I liked this new feeling, for they were now crying tears of joy and both hugging me between them. Whatever had happened to make them publicly show their love for me for all these people to see? And who were these people anyway, in their police cars, fire trucks, and an ambulance? Plus, traffic was backed up in both directions as far as the eye could see. Hey, what's going on here? That's what I wondered, when a policeman came over to my parents and my dad said, "Here she is! It wasn't her, thank God!" Tears were still running down his face.

"I'm glad," said the policeman. He continued, "Now we'll have to investigate to find out who she was."

What in the world were they talking about?! Just then, a neighbor lady from further up the road came running past the police who were holding the curious crowd back, and then I heard the saddest sound I would ever hear. At first she screamed, as a policeman talked to her. Then she started moaning over and over, "No … no … no …" That's when my parents decided to leave the scene, and they took me into our home, still being carried by my dad. Whatever had happened made me realize my dad sure did like me, and love me, too!

Returning from various places in the area to find a tragic event had occurred in front of their home, my brothers were with me when Dad told the story of what happened, and Mom gave us all milk and chocolate chip cookies.

First, our dad explained how the sirens had woken him, and he had hurriedly dressed and gone outside to see what had happened. My mom had joined him, and what they both saw was horrible and devastating. A huge truck with a trailer fully loaded had hit a little girl who had tried to run across the road in front of its tons of weight, moving at least sixty miles an hour. The driver had tried to stop, but at that speed, load and distance, it was impossible. The truck hit the child with such tremendous force, that her body had exploded into unidentifiable pieces, and had to be picked up with shovels and put into a large bushel. The firemen were doing that awful job.

"At first," Dad said, "we thought it was Betty Jean!"

No wonder they were so glad to see me! They thought I had been killed by a truck! Well, that certainly explained their joy in seeing me, and their good mood now! The whole family seemed really glad I was alive and that made me very happy. But that night, as Mom tucked us into bed and Dad stood in the doorway smiling, I suddenly thought of the little girl who had been killed and how very sad her family must feel. My mom must have read my mind, for as we said our regular prayer, she added some words. Our regular family prayer was:

Good night, Dear God,

We thank you for everything.

Please take care of us, this night and always, and help us always.

Help our dad in his work and our mom in hers, and keep us well and happy.

Help us to be good, and kind, and brave, and honest.

Good night, Dear God, grant peace to the world, through kindness and consideration, Amen.

Then my mother said, "Thank you, Dear God, for keeping our family safe. Please help the family of that child who was killed today. Please soothe their loss and help heal their suffering. And please help heal the truck driver whose spirit was broken today. Please restore their spirit so that goodness and happiness can return to them, someday. And Dear God, please welcome the child to your everlasting beauty and joy. Amen."

After the prayer was finished, I looked over at my dad and he again had tears running down his face. To me, he was the nicest dad in the world, at that moment. As I drifted off to sleep, I dreamed of a little girl, laughing and playing in a wondrous place with angels. The place had a familiar fragrance in my dream. Then I knew ... yes, there were lilacs in heaven.

CHAPTER EIGHTEEN

One evening when supper was over, Bobby, Donny and I decided to play "hide and seek" with Donny being "it." As he counted backwards from fifty, and we laughed because we knew he had a hard time counting frontwards to fifty, Bobby and I scurried through the house, seeking the best hiding places.

My parents' bedroom upstairs was empty, and the crib, which was in their room, was also empty. So I quickly climbed into the crib and pulled the blankets over me, thinking, "He'll never find me here!"

After a few minutes of listening for his movements as he searched through the house, I heard him approach the bathroom, and then I heard him remove the large metal lid on top of our big round clothes hamper, which my dad had custom-made. He must have been removing the top clothes, because I heard a yelp and laughing, and then it sounded like a herd of wild horses running down the stairs. Who reached the safety of home first, I'll never know, because just then I heard my father's serious voice saying, "Okay, enough of this noise! I'm going to try to get a few hours of sleep before I have to go to work, so everyone be quiet!"

Then I heard his footsteps coming up the stairs, and the next thing I knew, he was in the bedroom … the same bedroom where I was hiding in the crib! Not wanting to bring attention to myself, I decided just to stay where I was until he fell asleep, and then I would make my escape. A rustling sound came to my ears, and I realized he was undressing. Then I heard the sound of the crushing of the mattress springs as he got into his bed. As I waited patiently, not moving a muscle in my body, my fear was rising to my throat. No! I couldn't cough; he wasn't sleeping yet! The feeling passed and I managed to lie quietly in one spot, when suddenly my forehead started to itch. Darn those bangs; I needed another haircut! But I knew I had to ignore the itch, because, in the silence of the room, he would surely hear me scratching. It took all the power of my will to continue lying in that crib, motionless under those blankets.

As the minutes ticked by on the clock on the dresser, I started feeling very warm, and knew the blankets and my fear were going to roast me if he didn't hurry up and fall asleep! Just then I heard a soft snore, and then another one. After that, the snores came in louder cascades, one following the other, and I knew my dad was finally in a deep sleep.

Now I could make my escape! I gently pushed the blankets down off my sweating body, as I heard my brother Donny's voice in the distance asking, "Where's Betty Jean?" and Bobby answering, "I don't know!" with concern in his voice.

After the blankets were completely off of me, I lay there for another couple of minutes, just to make sure the snores were still coming. Then I sat upright and looked over toward my father's sleeping body. My eyes were adjusted to the darkness of the room, and I could see his body rise and fall with each snore. As I tried to pull myself to a standing position, so that I could swing my leg over the side of the crib and climb out, there was suddenly a huge explosion!

The crib mattress had broken and crashed to the floor, with me still in the crib, but now on the mattress on the floor! As I went down, my dad jumped up and yelled, "What's going on?!" in a scary booming voice!

Well, I didn't wait to explain … I just crawled out from under the crib and started running out of the room, with my dad in close pursuit! As I tore down the stairs, he was closing in on me and yelling what he was going to do to me as soon as he caught me! I ran for my life through the living room, with my brothers all looking at me and my dad chasing me in his long johns, and their faces looked quizzical with wonder. Of course, I didn't stop to explain, but ran around the corner and into the dining room, where I took a dive under the mahogany buffet. I could not have squeezed into a tighter ball in the corner of the wall under that buffet! From my position, I saw my dad's bare feet and heard him roar: "Where is she!?"

My eyes closed in self-defense; I figured if I couldn't see him, then he wouldn't see me! Just then, my mom came up from the basement to see what all the commotion was about, and she was able to calm him down and lead him back to bed.

Meanwhile, I opened my eyes and looked around. This was going to have to be my new home, I thought. I planned on sleeping in that corner and taking all my meals there, so that I could avoid the wrath of my dad. He had been so furious, that I just knew he must hate me, and I started to cry softly.

One by one my brothers came and got on their hands and knees to talk to me and calm me down from the "Dad attack." When they got it out of me exactly what had happened, they felt sorry for me and said that I had done the right thing, to wait for him to fall asleep. If only the crib hadn't broken so loudly, I would have been safe, they told me. They made me feel better, and then my mom came downstairs and looked under the buffet at her whimpering child.

"It'll be alright, Betty Jean. Tomorrow, you explain to your dad what happened and tell him you're sorry you disturbed his sleep, and he'll forgive you. He loves you, but you shocked him and he just reacted out of confusion. He's not mad anymore. He's sleeping again, so you can come out from under the buffet now. Don't be afraid, Honey … your dad would never hurt you."

As she said these words, I thought back on my life. She was right. He had never hurt us. All he did was yell, and that was enough to scare us. So I decided to leave the safety of the corner under the buffet and trust my mom to be right. And she was.

CHAPTER NINETEEN

The next day was my dad's day off, but it was also payday, and he had to go to the steel mill to pick up his paycheck. After I had gotten up the nerve to apologize and he had forgiven me, my mom was still concerned about our relationship, for she knew how angry he had been the night before, and she knew how terrified I had been. So she suggested to my dad that he take me with him to the steel mill to get his check.

"I don't know, Ann. The steel mill is not really the place where children belong," he said.

A steel mill! Wow! None of us kids had ever seen a steel mill! I would be the first, just like my hospital experience. Boy, did I ever want to go!

"I'll be really good, Dad, if you take me with you," I promised. "I'll do whatever you say, and I won't get in your way at all!" I was begging now. "Please, Dad!"

"All right," my dad agreed. "You can go with me if you want to. But promise to obey, so you don't get hurt!"

"I promise, Daddy."

After I got into the car and we were driving towards downtown Buffalo, a shyness descended on me, and I sat quietly, looking out the window at the passing scenery. There was the farm with the billy goats, and there was the fresh vegetable and fruit market. Soon, we were driving past my school, and my dad, sensing my quiet discomfort, broke the silence.

"Do you like school, Betty Jean?" he asked, politely.

"Oh yes!" I answered, enthusiastically.

"What subject do you like the most?" he asked.

We were on a roll here, I felt happily, as I responded, "My favorite subject is reading! And I really like reading about faraway places. It's called geography," I explained, just in case he had never heard of it.

"Oh, and I like when we have art or music! But we don't have them very often … maybe once a week. But I love when we draw or when we sing!"

This was good. For the first time in my life, I was having a conversation with my dad, and I felt happy.

"What subjects did you like when you were in school, Dad?" I asked, curious for the first time about his younger years, when he was just a boy and not my dad.

"Well, I liked math most of all. But I also liked reading and writing, especially penmanship, they called it then," he responded with a far-off look in his eyes, as though he had gone back in time to his boyhood.

He continued, "We used a series of books called the McGuffey Readers, and they sure were interesting. When we wrote, we used ink pens, which we dipped into a bottle of ink. The bottle sat in a hole on the right hand corner of the desk. Sometimes, writing with an ink pen got messy, but I liked it."

He smiled as he reminisced, and I felt a nice warm feeling come over me as I realized I would have liked to have known my dad as a boy.

The passing scenery had changed dramatically during our conversation. The farms had changed into just houses, and then we passed stores, restaurants, the hospital, and finally we were driving past a dirty section with big furnaces spewing colorful fire, smoke and sparks into the air.

As my dad slowed the big blue car down, we passed a large sign that I read: Bethlehem Steel. Then he turned in and drove past industrial buildings, and finally, he parked in a large parking lot that seemed filled with cars of all kinds. He told me to stay in the car until he came around and opened my door.

As I climbed out of the car, he took my hand and led me through the parking area.

"There sure are a lot of different kinds of cars," I said, and he agreed, as he started pointing at the various cars we walked past, and identifying them.

"This one is a Chevrolet, and that red one is a Ford. And here is a Buick, and over here, that yellow one is a Pontiac. This little green one is a Nash and that black one is a Chrysler. And this black one is a Studebaker."

My mind was trying to take it all in and remember what each car was, when I noticed that our car looked different from these, so I asked, "What kind of car do we have, Dad?"

He seemed to like my question as he happily responded, "We have a wonderful car called a Packard. It's nice and large enough for our family." He seemed proud of his choice of a car, which made me proud too.

Just then, a large dark presence blocked out the sun, and as we approached the opening of a gigantic complex, I felt a certain apprehension, and my dad and I stopped to look up at what was in front of us. My dad started explaining to me the different parts of the steel mill that we were seeing.

He told me that the brick building on the right was where the business office was located. On the left was a smaller building which was the payroll office. Behind that rose a series of towering blast furnaces, that he said took coal from the trains and combined it with other materials to make steel sheets, slabs, or ingots. I felt so small looking up at the giant structures in front of me that had twisted, intricate pipes spewing fire and billowing smoke.

Seeing all those cars in the parking lot made me realize my dad worked in an important industry that employed a lot of people. My dad smiled down at me before we entered the front gate and said, "Are you ready, Betty Jean? Here we go!" I took a big breath and held his hand tightly and nodded bravely—I was ready—and I could hardly wait to go inside.

But the first thing my dad did after we entered was to lead me over to an area with benches against the wall, and a box resting on the floor. He picked up a newspaper that someone had left lying on a bench, and he spread it on the floor near the box.

As I approached the box, I thought I heard what was in it, before I saw what was in it. I heard the sound of meowing. The box was filled with kittens ... seven kittens, to by exact! Oh boy, were they ever adorable!

"Sit on the newspaper and take one out at a time," my dad instructed. "After you're done petting one, put it back into the box before you take out another, okay?" he asked, talking loudly.

"Okay, Dad!" I loudly replied, as I sat on the newspaper on the floor and gently picked up a grey little fur ball. It was so soft and cute! It purred and really seemed to like sitting in my lap, as I caressed its soft fur. I felt like I was in heaven!

Then my dad spoke with an official tone in his voice as he instructed me: "Betty Jean, stay right there next to that box while I go to the office to get my paycheck. I'll be right back in a few minutes." Again, he spoke loudly, to be heard above the noise.

"Alright, Dad. I'll stay right here and play with the kittens!"

As he walked away, I looked back to my lap and noticed the grey kitten falling asleep, so I carefully picked him up and placed him back into the box. I checked out the remaining six kittens, and decided to pick up a coal black one next. He had yellow eyes and a playful disposition, as he tried to leave my lap. I captured him and put him back into the box, as I picked up a white kitten with green eyes. This kitten seemed really special for some reason, and I petted her gently.

Just then we were both startled by a loud noise, and for the first time, I stopped paying attention to the kittens and started looking around at my surroundings. It was a warm spring day outside, but for the first time I noticed the intense heat of this place. Then I noticed the sound; men had to yell to be heard, for there was so much loud noise. And filthy dirt with sort of sparkles in it coated everything. Then I saw a huge bucket tilt and start pouring a glowing whitish-yellow thick liquid that exploded bright sparks as it poured into another big bucket. All the working men knew their jobs, and as I watched in fascination, I saw the formation of glowing slabs moving along, and some men with torches were burning the slabs. As I continued to watch, I noticed how sparks flew up and burned the men's clothing, and even though it was extremely hot in that place, the men wore several layers of dirty, grimy clothes. The furnaces were roaring and colorful fireworks were shooting from the tops. It smelled like carbon, it smelled like fire, it smelled like burning! Amazed at

what I was witnessing, it dawned on me what this terrible place reminded me of … hell. If there were a hell on earth, it would be a steel mill! Being there for only a few minutes made me nauseous, yet my dad and all of these men had to come here every day for at least eight hours, and work in this terribly dangerous, dirty, deafening awful place.

Suddenly, I had a moment of enlightenment: my dad wasn't mean … he was just tired! While we were all sleeping all night long in our comfortable beds, he was here, in this dreadful place, working all night long, making steel for our country's needs. And he never complained about how hard his job was. All we knew was that he left each night and returned each morning. I never imagined what his hours in between his going and coming involved. My dad worked in hell! Because he loved his family, he put his life on the line each night in order to support us. All he ever needed from us was quiet, so that he could sleep in the day, in order to get his strength back for the next night's work.

Oh no! How inconsiderate we've all been through these years, never once thinking of our father's needs, and just thinking he's mean! Well, as soon as I get home, I thought to myself, I'm going to tell the family what I've learned today: if our dad works in hell all night long, then we owe it to him to make his home as much like heaven as we possibly can. At least I knew we had to make the effort, for his sake.

As I saw him approaching, I smiled at him and he smiled back at me. When he was standing above me, he saw the white kitten in my lap and said loudly, "Would you like to take one of the kittens home? Which one do you want to join our family?"

I couldn't believe my ears, even though he had shouted the words, in order for me to hear him above the sounds of hell. Sure, I wanted to take one home! I looked into the box at all the various color combination of kittens. Then I looked at the white one in my lap, looking up at me with the sweetest expression, as though saying: "Pick me!" So that's the one I picked!

As we were walking back through the parking lot, I asked my dad a question: "Dad, what do you do in the steel mill? What's your job?"

Again he looked at me with a smile, as though he was pleased with my curiosity, and he answered, "What's my job? That's a very good question, Betty Jean. Well, my title is 'Foreman,' which means I'm the boss of my shift ... the night shift. My job is to make steel by supervising the process, so that the final product ... the steel ... is perfect, but more importantly, my job is to see that everything my workers do to make that steel is done safely, to ensure that no one gets hurt, or even killed, because, as you saw, a steel mill is a very dangerous place. Through the years, before people recognized the importance of having a safe workplace, many men were killed in the steel mills. Now there are rules and safety inspectors, but every so often an accident will happen. My job is to make sure it never happens on my shift."

Gee, my dad was a boss! But even if he had been one of the regular workers, I still would be proud of him! In school we had learned about all the things made out of steel, and how important the industry was ... and my dad was a part of that industry!

There was one more question I needed to ask him as we neared where our Packard was parked. So I asked, "Dad, why are kittens in a steel mill?"

He responded in a matter-of-fact way by saying, "Well, it's not so much that kittens are in the steel mill, but their moms and dads are important. You see, Honey, steel mills are filthy places with rats running around trying to eat the food in workers' lunches. So the mill has cats to take care of the rats, and the cats have kittens. Therefore, that's why kittens are in the steel mill." Made sense to me!

After we left the mill and were driving home, my dad was busy maneuvering through traffic, and I sat contentedly caressing my new little friend. My dad looked over at us and laughed, as he exclaimed, "For a moment there, when I looked at you, it looked like you had a snowball in your lap, Honey!"

That's when we both realized he had just named our new kitten: Snowball. What a perfect name for a perfect kitten!

As we arrived home, the whole family happened to be there, and everyone was thrilled with the new addition. From now on, even in the summer, we had a Snowball!

When my brothers asked what the steel mill had been like, I answered, "It was like hell!"

"Betty Jean!" My mom was shocked. "We don't use that kind of language!"

But my dad interrupted her correction with these words: "Betty Jean is exactly right. She's not saying a bad word; she's telling the truth. Working in the steel mill is like working in hell! She's just describing what she saw today."

That's when I offered my nice dad an apology from all of us: "Daddy, I'm so sorry we haven't been good and quiet so you could get the sleep you need each day. From now on, we should all do our best to keep things quiet while Dad sleeps, because he really needs a good day's rest to be able to work each night in that terrible place, while we all sleep."

One by one, my brothers agreed, and that was the beginning of a new era for our family. But on Dad's days off, we were our old exuberant, noisy, boisterous brothers with their side-kick sister, having adventures galore!

EPILOGUE

After five years in Buffalo, we moved back to Ohio, where my dad got another job as a foreman, again working in a steel mill. As usual, we kids had new horizons to explore!

Many years passed and we all grew up with families of our own, when one day, my son, David, an inventor and welder, was buying supplies at an industrial warehouse. At the exit was a massive old steel gear, and he stopped and stared at it, mesmerized by its size, purpose, and what it represented. Suddenly, he felt his grandpa's presence as he examined the giant gear. He had known about his grandpa working in the steel mills, but standing before that huge gear put a new perspective on that awareness.

As he stared at the gear, he felt a profound respect for the maker of such things so basic, yet complicated, and he realized the great contribution his grandpa, his dad, and all the people who worked in the steel mills, had made to the building of our modern, civilized world. Then he felt an immense sense of pride and gratitude.

As David drove home that afternoon, a song came on the car radio, titled "True Colors," and as he listened to the meaningful words, he looked toward where the sun had just appeared from behind the clouds. But it wasn't the sun alone that was in the sky that afternoon, for a beautiful rainbow was circling the sun, filled with vibrant colors. Again, he felt his grandpa's spirit, and as the words of the song continued, he wondered about the colors of his grandpa's life. What had been his grandpa's talents, his dreams, his aspirations? In the need to provide for his family by working in an extremely hard, unglamorous industry, did his grandpa even have the energy to dream and to let his true colors show? Or had his life been shades of dreary grey in the struggle to survive during difficult times? If his grandpa had been born in other circumstances, and had the privilege of having opportunities to choose, what choices would he have made? Would he have chosen a literary life, or have been an artist? Or would he have been a great musician, or business leader? Or maybe a doctor, or an astronomer, or an airline pilot? As the song ended, he realized that his grandpa Streb and the hundreds of thousands of steelworkers were responsible for making the raw materials that made everything he was seeing from the highway: the steel beams supporting the bridge, all the cars and trucks on the roads, all the steel signs, the buildings in the downtown skyline, and even the huge television/radio tower soaring into the colorful sky. As he glanced at the sky, he sensed his grandparents' presence in the two faint but glorious rainbows on both sides of the sun. David began to feel a connection to my childhood and a need to learn more about my dad.

So when he walked into our home and joined me in the family room, he told me about his sensing his grandpa's spirit as he had stared at the giant steel gear. He told me how he had listened to a song about a person's true colors as he drove home. Then he said to me, "Tell me about when you moved to Buffalo, New York, as a child, and your dad worked at the steel mill."

Glad to share my memories, I began: "When I was a child, I thought my dad was so mean. But let me start at the beginning … It should be against the law. In fact, it probably was. But my dad did it anyway … he picked me up and hung me over the rail at Niagara Falls …"

About the Author

Elizabeth Streb Parks has authored three books: *My Dad Was So Mean*, and the children's books, *Kevie Keanu's Walk With Nana* and *David's Castle On Crescent Beach*, co-authored with her son, David Phillip Parks, who also illustrated her books. Living in several states (Ohio, New York, Arizona, California, Florida and Hawaii) she appreciates the beauty and diversity of the people and places in North America. Early in her career, she was a telephone operator in three states, and owned a bakery in Arizona. After Majoring in Real Estate at a state university, she was a Realtor at two companies in Ohio. As a life-long learner, she has done television commercials for her local library, since her love of reading started there. (Her picture is on both sides of a large library delivery truck!)

When she encountered the two roads diverged in a yellow wood, she didn't take either road, but instead blazed a new trail through the woods and to the beach. Her journey of adventure and serendipity, with her husband, two children and grandson has been a blessing from the universe.

About the Illustrator

David Phillip Parks is the author/illustrator of the children's books, "Living In Flohio" and "Weather … It Matters," the co-author (with Elizabeth Streb Parks) and illustrator of "David's Castle On Crescent Beach," the illustrator of Elizabeth Streb Parks' books, "Kevie Keanu's Walk With Nana" and "My Dad Was So Mean," co-author (with Marlene McKnight Koenig) and illustrator of "Frisky Wins His Heart."

Besides writing/illustrating, David's involved in a variety of pursuits: plays several musical instruments (mainly drums), inventing/applied mechanical engineering, welding/metal-working, athletics and nature. Having lived in both Ohio and Florida, he studied at a state university and is a Meteorologist/storm spotter, specializing in severe weather and field research in tornado development.

www.ingramcontent.com/pod-product-compliance
Lightning Source LLC
Chambersburg PA
CBHW041508220426
43661CB00017B/1285